These Indiana Winters
By B. T. Roen

These Indiana Winters

B. T. Roen

Published by B. T. Roen, 2024.

While every precaution has been taken in the preparation of this book, the publisher assumes no responsibility for errors or omissions, or for damages resulting from the use of the information contained herein.

THESE INDIANA WINTERS

First edition. October 28, 2024.

ISBN: 979-8227417985

Written by B. T. Roen.

Table of Contents

To my mother & father, who always saw the poetry in
me

These Indiana Winters

So cold, with
water in the air, even
the water heater wears
a scarf riveted
around red pipes
and yarn lines
shiver inside
the building's skin
isn't too thin—
lets the little sun in—
but it's too thin
to keep the heat in
lead on, they said
keep on the lid
anger cooled is
pressurized
depression
'tis the season
bleaking dreams in-
side my head
seeing paint
on peeling lead
My only happy

holidays are
past and future
thread my newest
scarf with suture
stitch my joy
inside my heart again
give back my scarf
and pipes of red.

Laundry In The Rain

Reflecting on the time my family lived in a converted garage on a
Midwest campground
It's nice to have an indoor laundry room.
For once.
We used to walk outside,
around the house,
and in the back
to wash our clothes
Dodging racoons drunk on some
fermented mushroom,
leaving the puppy inside
quaking at barred owls' cries
yipping for our return
It wasn't bad on the way there.
We just hoped the rain would stop
before the dryer was done.

My Mother's House Plants

its roots wherever it can bloom
no need for water—
her love sustains all
the pots have moved seventeen times
never cracked or chipped, at home
in box and home and moving truck,
just like her unwavering love
Thorns wisp fronds of jade,
spill potted pottery in green
limes round their bending branches
wait for aloe's soothing mother-touch
clean air in corners crooked
for heads and hearts
join branches with the family tree
that brought you to new roots.

Advice My Dad Received As A Young Pastor

Pack your bags
to stay forever
ready for the next move
Within a year,
Attend at least
A single strong strategic funeral
Stretch your patience
dodge the politics
of carpet color and Kool-Aid
Remember your call
to this human flock
and love them all the same.

Children Don't Pray

They sit quietly in the pew
Better yet, they're shuffled off
from holy toils
stuffed into Sunday School boxes
out of mind
so the adults can access heaven.
They do not pray for themselves
They do not pray for others
And they certainly do not cross the sanctuary
to hug a weeping stranger
Lest they make me feel callous,
cribbed, confined within my self-selection
for heaven's comfort
I could not deign to touch a suffering soul
For fear their grief might wake my empathy
or worse, their grief reminds me of my own
stacked like bones behind my closet door
never to be mentioned anymore...
No. Children should not pray.
The world is far too full of suffering
to let their love attempt to heal a bit.

Real People Waterski

therefore, I was not a real people
to my great uncle
we didn't really talk much anyway
I drifted away to take point in the bow,
content to see my mother's joy
as she cut across the motorboat's wake,
her beautiful strength like a lighthouse
guiding me to independence.
Real people know what *Sleeping Beauty* is
therefore, I was not a real people
in the eyes of quite a few adults and peers.
They mocked my "missing childhood"
before I knew what it meant to be
transgender, looking back on
childhood clothes meant for a different closet.
Real people get a "real job"
therefore, I am not a real people
despite coming of age onstage
taxes don't care what I do, why should you?
I've stayed my inner child
kept them waiting for love
in the name of practicality.
Real people...

Real people...
Real *people*...
I un-advice my childhood
find myself
in echoes

Jumping Contest With Jack Frost in Celery Bog

I lost.

At first,
I kept pace
flipping over fractals
and frozen fronds of bark

He twirled up a tree,
small snow shadows
dancing in branches,
barking brittle cackles

I followed:

> slick
> slack
> *snap—*

cold ground is hard.

I Walk Outside The Agate Tree (A Faerie's Lament)

I walk outside the agate tree
in spots and stars of wingless gold
to hide away my neighbors here
in tales and trees of timeless old.
My neighbors fought for safety there,
before they came to live with me,
for Duke Malere will hunt them down
for made-up crimes of vagrancy
I spun a fog around his home,
in hopes of keeping him at bay,
but what will make him finally stop?
I fear that only time can say.

Turtle Talks To Tree

and asks slowly,

How is your day?

A shadow of the
beautiful cycle,
(says the tree*)
Life
is like a bookshelf.
Empty at the start,
built from kindred's heart,
slowly filling with
adventure,
heartbreak,
heart-make,
losing,
laughing,
wonder,
wish,
suspense,
thrill,
friends,
villains,

family,
stories,
Life.

*The tree later apologized to the turtle for monopolizing the
page.

Can Porcupines Pop Popcorn?

Can birds
burst balloons?
Do bears
blow bubblegum?
Do salmon
sip soda?

Maybe.

If bushes
burst into salty snow with passing friction
If leaves
inflated and caught on branches
If roars
grew shields that a pin could puncture
If rivers
fizzed with carbon-color

maybe Some of these things are already true.

Can humans live like porcupines?
birds?
bears?
salmon?

Maybe. If they

climb,
fly,

run,
swim—

Some of these must grow to be true.

Your 6pm Midwestern Gender Forecast

Today is cloudy with a 60% chance of
feminine showers. Pad your inner child with
barefoot reassurances: this rain will pass,
pressure will drop, you will weather it all.
Tonight, temperatures will drop
slower than a voice on T—
we could freeze into gendersolid by 3AM.
Over the weekend, bring out the black hoodies:
we're looking at a 90% chance of enby
with masculine gusts up to 35 binders per hour.
Highs in the gender euphoria might send you
airborne with rebirthed self-love, while
lows in anxiety and accidental "ma'am"s
could result in black-ice depression.
Next week looks mild, with a few days of
sunny skies and calm agender vibes.
But, like we always say in Indiana:
if you don't like the gender,
wait five minutes.
Stay safe out there.

Pocket Check

My mother says I look
like Columbo, though
my pen usually perches
behind my ear
Tap, pat, tap, pat
mirror-image words
tell me each pocket
has its proper contents
it's a habit from the before
days, when I was trapped
with half-inch fake seams
teasing closed-up jeans storage
when I came out, I went in
to thrift store boys' sections
relishing freedom contained
in pockets bigger than fists
now everything has its home
right/left hip/thigh, who knew
my gender would find its home
in the pockets of my cargo pants

Playing Cornhole At a Bar With Scottish Actors

I love swapping stories and dialects
for work: no cubicles for me
unless an audience is the fourth wall.
I love that "networking" for me
is playing cornhole
at midnight
at a bar
with Scottish actors.

I do not love that cornhole set.
Beanbags just a bit too heavy,
boards just a bit too slick—
a bigger test of skill than I expected
at midnight
at a bar
with Scottish actors.

They had the excuse of novelty and beer
on their side.
One actress gave it a go
scored a three pointer
at least once
almost every round.
I grew up on the game

25

and don't drink...
I never landed a single shot
at midnight
at a bar
with Scottish actors.

Identi-"he"

unsought-for twinkle of gender joy
born in my roommate's apology-laugh
when she switched a he/him
for my they/them in a story
I froze on a spiraling what-if
wave through my heart,
happy as when it joyed in "they"
At first, I thought it a mistake:
just a funny story, no epiphany.
my fear-hobbled realization
tiptoed from self-doubt shadows
to my heart's door, pulling
the string of my heart's bell, whose
chime rang ever so softly: *he is you:*
he and they are equally true.

Being Non-Binary is Like Being Graupel

Most folks experience your existence,
see you in their lives, or hear of you
by reputation, though Mainstream
claims not to know your history.
The experts acknowledge your true name
But some, a small handful refuse,
apply their own reality with closed-off ears,
Lump you in with hail or snow
You're neither; a separate space
On the precipitation spectrum:
Softer than hail, sharper than rain
A not-quite-sleet lookalike—
Some say you're cheating.
Pretending, grooming rain
Into a life-altering decision to freeze
Against its wishes
But you only befriend the raindrops
Who choose to be with you.
You stay above freezing, asking
For friendship, and the clouds answer.

Hail is just really angry snow

Tossed and battered around
tested for weight
The clouds use hail in volleyball contests:
Drop it to the ground to melt
as soon as they're bored
No wonder hail grows up feeling useless.
Nobody goes out to play in hail—
They run and hide,
curse its damage,
greet kings with its destructiveness
Hail screams to be heard
as it shatters glass birds:
"LOVE ME for once!
Melt my heart with a
warm embrace
return me to my
waters' home."
When all hail heals,
perhaps, so will we.

Snow Day Whitecaps

foam roils out of fog, churning
white from grey nowheres—
like the time I joked that a friend didn't like me
they stopped,

    "lies!" they said,
    kind and constant as the morning sun
    that should've been the end of it
    but the memory churns like wind-whipped waves
    day and night: "why did I say that?"

snowflakes whirl in anxiety spirals
the lake disappears from the sky
like my confidence when I think of their face
did they really think I was joking?
day and night: "why did I say that?"
the trees fade, but don't quite disappear
though the snow tries to block them out
like their care for me despite
my one remark: staying
late to find my missing mitten
the lake, blanket of tranquility, reappears
solid, steady life-line in waves

like my self-confidence-love-
judgment-criticism-respect-
assurance-confidence-love
day and night: "I said what I feared,
I heard what I loved."

Being Non-Binary is Natural Selection Doing Its Darndest to Be Beautiful

It's tough driving evolution

    the car's always running
    off the tracks!

Slicing between rock and rushes
like a knife that's divorced itself

    from its wielder

mutilating creation with stagnation:
a suffocation of change
reveals the sanctuary we lost
in the realm of curiosity
Gender roles stain glass
with queer blood
dams stop the river of life,
lock it in lakes of complacency
The car drives a straight line, but
Earth offers queer kinds of roads:
more paths than strands

on a spiderweb.

The car is not life's only transport,
though it tries to kill the rest.
It plows through squirrel and fowl,
flattens bush and brier.
But it cannot win against the
running deer, the soaring eagle,
the floating branch upon the waves,
the whales underneath the sea.

THESE INDIANA WINTERS

The car will find itself upon a cliff,
            teetering between the options left:
refuse to yield and dive into its death, or learn to live with life
instead of rule,
relinquishing machined (in)"security"
for nature's unpredictability.

A Dance Unseen

Great stubborn roots of self-doubt frost
melt all away to nothing
the music whisks your soul aloft
for smiles and for loving
Though trees may speak when no one hears,
when they fall all alone,
the dusty witness to felled freedom
dances on its own.

40

Being Non-Binary Is Like A Walk In The Park

Paths are guidelines, not obligations.
The world unfolds its petals—
explore and celebrate!—
adds a color, shade, feather, leaf
scale is in the eye of the beholder.
mushrooms of a thousand genders
usher new life from death
a robin— half male, half female—
has two fathers, grows up to wife a wife
a person transitions to parent:
They save orphans, following the
queerness of natural tradition.

42

Golden Days

Responding to Rattle's Ekphrastic August 2023 prompt
I dream of future golden days
preparing for nostalgia's gold-wash
glow upon my memories of dreams:
My mother sits at the desk my father made,
picture-image of her grandmother,
mending my nephew's
costume for the school play
He's playing his first lead:
Prince Hal in *Henry IV*.
Defending himself in rehearsal,
he ripped his poet's blouse,
coming out to my mother and I
as he held the sundered pieces of his tears,
my mother held his heart in one hand,
teaching him to weave the threads of
love and curiosity with the other.
He's gone playing now, and my mother stitches:
clothes are how she shows her love.
She writes his pronouns on the tag
with silk as variegated as his self-discovery:
every tear makes room for new lines to color through
The sun sets through her window,

shows the halo set in her white curls;
she sews my new nephew's blouse:
our guardian angel in glasses.

That Summer Was An Endless Season of Our Innocence

That summer was an endless season of
our innocence. The egg was waiting, still,
to crack was not to be: for now, to sleep.
To sleep, be safe, and dream again the dream
that would not wake until we left for school
the dream that echoed ever in our mind
and rose to fill itself in joy again
when distance would become our closest friend.
To wait until we had the time to stop,
to stop, perchance, to think. To think, and know
that former selves are not invalid in
their ignorance, but live to tell a part
of our young history. Our story still
has time to spin, to weave around again
in newer understandings of itself.

To The Six-Year-Old Me

To the six year old me
who's wondering
why you can't run like the boys
in just a pair of swim trunks
It's because you are
a different kind of boy
a changeling child who never left home
a boy who hasn't woken up yet

There Is Such A Thing

as too much empathy
borrowing baggage that leaves you
lying on the couch
stomach rumbling to the
rhythm of another's grumbling
You were never meant
to pick this up:
not your room,
not your vacuum.
A bag on sale
is not an obligation to buy.
If someone tries to sell you
their baggage, you refuse.
So why would you choose
what's there for free?
It weighs twice as much.
This choice has become a reflex
an influx of reflux
claiming emotional vomit as your own—
you don't even see what's yours
until its bubbles paralyze your appetite
one stomach can't hold
that much muck.

Let gravity do its job
bring baggage to the abyss
and leave you the lighter
for the loss.

Time Flies When You're Having Fun

Whooping through the air
like if Icarus got a happy ending
Time does that, you know,
Because joy is lighter than Grief,
certainly, both are lighter than
hate.
Time carries Grief for as long as you do;
their patience lasts as long as it is healthy.
Hate and Time have never gotten along.
They bind each other as
Hate grinds the natural order—
the glue-shield of families,
the parachute-picnic of friends,
humanity's mycorrhizal network: Love—
into twists of toxicity.
Time and Love and Joy are patient.
Faith and Patience guide them,
tiptoeing into subtext
drifting into drips of dull
everydayness.
That's how they get you.
While Time distracts you with their
aerial loop-de-loops,

you slowly remember to smile again.

Don't miss out!

Visit the website below and you can sign up to receive emails whenever B. T. Roen publishes a new book. There's no charge and no obligation.

https://books2read.com/r/B-A-GUQQC-FQYDF

BOOKS 2 READ

Connecting independent readers to independent writers.

Also by B. T. Roen

These Indiana Winters

Watch for more at https://www.bekstrythfreeman.com/.

About the Author

Beks Roen (they/he) is a queer Shakespeare nerd & sword-wielding chaos goblin from Indiana focused on adventurous connection. He uses his acting, writing and teaching skills to show people they're not alone. They founded Blanket Fort Theatre in 2024, dedicating their career to highlight queer joy, stage combat, & Shakespeare fun across the Midwest. An internationally published poet, Roen's work can be seen in The NonBinary Review, Querencia Press, Beyond the Veil Press, Anodyne Magazine & more. In theatre, Beks has worked with Great Lakes Theater, Purdue Theatre, the Hoosier Shakespeare Festival, the Civic Theatre of Greater Lafayette, the Hudson Valley Shakespeare Festival, & more.

Read more at https://www.bekstrythfreeman.com/.

www.ingramcontent.com/pod-product-compliance
Lightning Source LLC
Chambersburg PA
CBHW061405140726
47997CB00003B/1377